To
....

We're going to
....

From
....

Instagram: Creabooks
creabookspublishings@gmail.com

Copyright @ Creabookspublishings
all rights reserved

Thank you for purchasing!

Want a freebie?

Leave a review for your amazon purchase & contact us via instagram or email!

Check out our huge range of Books at http://tiny.cc/Creabooks

Instagram: Creabooks
creabookspublishings@gmail.com

Copyright © Creabookspublishings
all rights reserved

Printed in Dunstable, United Kingdom

64697045R00030